3 Day Guide to Santorini

A 72-hour definitive guide on what to see, eat and enjoy in Santorini, Greece

3 DAY GUIDES

ISBN: 1506190979
ISBN-13: 978-1506190976

"Travel makes one modest. You see what a tiny place you occupy in the world." – Scott Cameron

CONTENTS

1 INTRODUCTION TO SANTORINI

Santorini, Greece. Photo credit: Nicholas Doumani

Santorini (Thira) is a charming and surreal
Mediterranean paradise that may have conquered
your imaginations before you have even laid eyes
on it. Touted as the most beautiful island in the
Greek island group, Cyclades, this scintillating
destination is famous for its extraordinary scenery,
intriguing history, sapphire waters and starry-eyed
setting.

A sightseer's nirvana, the island bombards its

tourists with its majestic sights, such as Oia's legendary sunsets and breathtaking hilltop village. Photography enthusiasts will be amazed with the astonishing sugar-cube buildings fastened on the gorgeous 400-meter cliffs of the caldera in Fir, the island's capital. A marriage of Cycladic and Venetian architecture, Fira also has dazzling immaculate white cobblestone streets buzzing with cafes, shops, hotels and tavernas.

Are you a beach bum? Then, you surely are in for a treat on this picturesque volcanic island. While beaches aren't Santorini's biggest tourist draws, it still has a wide collection of beaches to keep you hooked and entertained for days. With its deep blue waters and awe-inspiring rock formation, these beaches would certainly give you a taste of heaven on earth.

What makes these beaches really stand out, though, is their mysterious and one-of-a-kind ambiance. Influenced by the island's volcanic nature, these beaches feature a fascinating blend of spectacular steep cliffs, crystal clear sapphire waters and red volcanic pebbles. The island also serves as a home to some of the country's most popular nude beaches, such as Vlychada and Kamari.

Fond of sightseeing? Do you love taking snapshots of beautiful architectural gems? As a tourist in this wonderful Mediterranean wonderland, you will have endless of opportunities for sightseeing as well as taking selfies with eye-catching buildings and houses on the background. Famed for its blue-domed churches and   white-washed homes, Oia and Fira (two of the island's most popular hot spots) are speckled with dainty pastel-colored building perched on the caldera's cliffs. What's more, the island has unspoiled seascape and landscapes, making it one of the world's great natural wonders.

The island of Santorini has no shortage of archaeological sites and historic landmarks. After all, Greece is the cradle of civilization in the western world. Tourists will be bombarded with a myriad of intriguing historic sites, from the Ancient Thera and Akrotiri to the Byzantine Castle Ruins and La Ponta-Venetian Tower. In addition, the island boasts a pair of amazing history museums, namely the Archaeological Museum and the Museum of Prehistoric Thira.

Are you a foodie? This beautiful island will treat all your gastronomic urges with its ambrosial culinary offerings like the auberigine (an odd-looking eggplant), fried tomato balls and fava caper. For wine connoisseurs, Thira has a host of local wineries that offer sumptuous white grape varieties like Aidani, Athiri and Assyrtiko.

Santorini is arguably the most beautiful and romantic destination in all of Greece. With its splendid scenery and astonishing sunsets, couples won't find it difficult to feel the romance of this laid-back paradise. As a matter of fact, hordes of newlyweds and couples flock to this island just to experience its tranquil, exquisite and romantic ambiance. Like a couple struck by Cupid's arrow, the island's nostalgic feel will surely make you fall in love all over again with your other half.

So, if you are planning on going on a honeymoon or looking for an idyllic respite to rekindle your romance with your other half, don't forget to include Santorini to your list of destination choices.

History

Are you familiar with the mythical Greek island known as Atlantis? Well, Santorini is believed to be the site of this storied magical island. But sadly, everyone knows this spellbinding island really never existed. Despite all the presented vulcanological and archeological evidence linking the island to the myth, historians and scientists still believe that Atlantis is just a pigment of Plato's imagination. Nevertheless, the island of Santorini has a very long and colorful history that would captivate historians and any typical tourist.

In ancient times, this charming Greek island was a round and single island known as Strongili. During those times, the island's inhabitants were quite influential in the area, and shared a lot of traits with Crete's Minoans. But in 1,500 BC, the massive volcano underneath the island erupted with a herculean force that made the island's center a sunken crater. What's more, its explosion caused colossal tidal waves and changed the weather conditions of the island. Known as one of the biggest volcanic eruptions in human history, this eruption is often considered the cause of destruction of the Minoan civilization. Also, it was responsible for the creation of an enormous underwater caldera surrounded by islands, which are known collectively as the Cyclades group of islands.

By the way, a lot of Greeks think that the sinking of Santorini's center is related to the destruction of Atlantis. Also, some historians assumed that the island's eruption has a connection to the Biblical plagues of Egypt in the Book of Exodus.

In 1,300 BC, the island was occupied by Phoenicians, who stayed there for five generations. In 1,115 BC, the island of Santorini was colonized by an ancient Greek civilization known as Lacedaemonia. The island's inhabitants eventually baptized the island as 'Thera' around 825 BC, while using Phoenician alphabet. In the 6th and 7th centuries BC, the island had flourishing trade and commercial relations with several cities and islands in Greece. In the midst of the Hellenistic Period, the island became an epicenter for naval base and trade, thanks to its perfect central location.

From 1200 to 1579, Thera was under the rule of the Byzantines, and the Episkopi Gonia church was founded. During 1204, Thera was surrendered to Marco Sanudo (a Venetian), becoming a part of the

Duchy of the Archipelago. The rulers, then, gave the name 'Santorini' to the island in honor of a Venetian catholic church known as Santa Irini. From 16th to 19th centuries, the island was under the Turkish rule. But in 1832, the island and the rest of Greece became independent from the Ottoman Empire after a successful uprising.

The island suffered a couple of major setbacks in the 20th century. During the Second World War, the island's economy declined significantly. Even worse, the island was abandoned by its inhabitants after a destructive earthquake in 1956. But in the 1970s, the government made great strides in making it an attractive honeymoon and holiday tourist destination. Today, Santorini is highly viewed as one of Greece's premier and most believed destinations.

Climate and seasons

With a fascinating blend of cool evening breeze and sun-filled days, it is no wonder a lot of travelers consider Santorini as one of the top travel destinations in the Mediterranean region. Furthermore, the island has a warmer and more pleasant year-round climate, as compared to other sought-after destinations in Europe. To top it all off, it has favorable sea temperatures that range from 60 to 70 degrees Fahrenheit (15 to 21 degrees Celsius).

When is the best time to visit this Mediterranean

paradise? The answer depends on your budget, preferences and choice of activities. To enjoy the ultimate sightseeing adventure in Santorini, you should visit the island during its tourist season, which starts from April (Easter) and ends on May. With mild temperatures that hover between 60 to 70 degrees Fahrenheit (15 to 21 degrees Celsius), Santorini's peak season is indeed the best time to gaze on the beautiful sights of the island. As expected, the island will be teeming with European and Greek visitors during this season.

How about swimming? The island's tourist season may not be a good time to wear a swimsuit, and explore the waters of Cyclades. But when summertime comes, Akrotiri's Red Beach and the island's other admirable beaches will be speckled with beach lovers.

From June to August, the island enjoys a warm and sunny summer season, with an average daily high of 80 degrees Fahrenheit (26 degrees Celsius), and cool night breezes in the 70-degree Fahrenheit range (21 degrees Celsius). Not to mention, tourists can experience 13 hours of sunshine during this season. Aside from its great warm weather, summertime also has a host of festivals and key events, including the Ifestia Festival, Profitis Ilias, Festival of Megaron Gyzi and Jazz Festival Santorini.

The Aegean waters are still pretty warm in the months, September and October. Also, during these months, tourists get to enjoy sunny days, with daytime temperatures ranging from 70 to 80 degrees Fahrenheit (21 to 26 degrees Celsius). Besides swimming, these months can be the perfect time to discover the majestic natural wonders and historic sites of Santorini as well. And thankfully, room rates drop drastically during this time, as these months attract fewer crowds.

The island's low season (November to March) is probably the least popular time to take a vacation in Satorini. With an average daily temperature of 50 degrees Fahrenheit (10 degrees Celsius), it is hardly pleasant to swim, sunbathe or do any beach activities during this season. On the bright side, the island's low season has the lowest rates for restaurants and lodging accommodations.

Language

The official language for this spectacular historic Mediterranean island is, obviously, Greek. If you have never been to Greece, or you are not fluent in Greek, try to bring an English-to-Greek dictionary with you. While most locals in Satorini speak or at least understand common English words, a dictionary can come in handy, especially if you are planning to explore Santorini's off beaten paths and secluded villages like Pyrgos and Vothonas.

Getting In

Did you know that Santorini has its own airport? Yes, you've heard it right. The island of Thira is one of the very few islands in the Cyclades archipelago with a major national airport. Nestled on the island's Kamari village, the Santorini National Airport caters regular flights from Greece's capital, Athens, through a trio of commercial airlines, including Aegan Airlines, Olympic Air, and a seaplane airline called AirSea Lines. From Athens to Thira, the flight duration usually takes thirty minutes. During summertime, Sky Express connects Thira with other sought-after Greek island destinations, such as Mykonos, Rhodes and Crete. In addition, Astra Airlines offers commercial flights from Thessaloniki during July and August.

Aside from commercial airlines, there are a few charter airlines that fly directly to Thira from several airports in Europe. But take note, charter flights to the island are only available from May to October. Anyway, below is a list of charter airlines that fly to this Greek arcadia.

- Transavia – Amsterdam

- Thompson – Manchester

- ThomasCook – Brussels, Manchester and London Gatwick

- SAS- Oslo

- Norwegian – Stockholm, Oslo and Copenhagen

- Meridiana – Milan Malpensa

- Jetairfly – Brussels

- Germanwings – Stuttgart, Munich, and Cologne

- Edelweiss Air –Zurich

- EasyJet – Milan Malpensa, Manchester, and London Gatwick

- Condor – Hamburg, Munich, Frankfurt, Stuttgart and Dusseldorf

- Air Berlin – Vienna, Nuremberg, Hamburg, Düsseldorf, Berlin Tegel

Taking a plane is, of course, a faster route than traveling by sea. Plus, it is a lot more convenient and comfortable, especially to tourists who suffer from sea sickness. Sadly, air tickets to this destination sell out quickly, particularly during the peak seasons. For those who prefer to get to Santorini by air, make sure to book your tickets a few months prior to your scheduled trip.

Can't catch a flight to the island Santorini? Then, go to Piraeus (Athens's ancient port), and hop on a car ferry bound to the island of Santorini. For the most part, a car ferry trip to the island of Santorini takes eight to ten hours, depending on the number of stops that the ferry makes. As for the price, each ferry ride costs 34 EUR per person.

Is there are a faster way to travel by sea to Thira? Thankfully, there are high-speed catamarans that would take you to the island in a faster fashion. For a reasonable price of 60 EUR a catamaran ride would take you to the island within five hours or less.

Getting Around

From walking to ATV rides, there are a lot of ways you can get around the island of Santorini. For adventuresome explorers, you should try to get around the island on foot. As you walk around the island, you will get to discover some of the island's hidden treasures as well as get up close and personal with the friendly and charming locals of the island. As a bonus, you get to behold and take pictures of several glorious Santorini landmarks and architectures, such as the picturesque streets of Pyrgos and the old Cycladic churches of Megalochori.

The perks of walking around the island go beyond enjoying the pretty sights of the island's seaside towns. With walking as your means of getting around Santorini, you get a chance to save a lot of money from your transportation costs during your Greek getaway or vacation. Not to mention, walking is fairly easy on the island, thanks to its winding and narrow roads as well as compact towns. Just make sure, though, to keep an eye for small motorized bikes, as they are allowed to travel on both the sidewalks and streets.

Taking a bus ride is probably the second best option, next to walking. After all, it is the only means of public transportation on the island.

Nonetheless, its local bus system is very efficient, extensive, reliable, and best of all, inexpensive. For an affordable price, a bus ride takes you to the island's most beloved towns and destinations like Perissa, Vourvoulus, Kamari and La.

Taxi cabs are available on both Thirassia and Thira. Rates for taxi cabs are fixed at 12 EUR, for major routes like Fira to Oia. If, however, you are using a taxi cab to get around the less-popular villages, make sure to come to terms upon a rate before getting inside the taxi cab.

While public buses are reliable and convenient, they can be often overcrowded during the peak season. As an alternative, tourists would rent cars, mopeds (small motorized bikes) and ATVs' (all-terrain vehicles). There are a few rental agencies for these vehicles in Fira as well as the airport. To drive any of these vehicles, however, you need to secure an international driver's license, which you can apply online at:

http://www.idlservice.com/

2 A TASTE OF THE CYCLADES CULTURE AND PAST

Clifftop Church in Fira - Santorini, Greece. Photo credit:
Kevin Poh

Do you want to experience the true essence of this
volcanic island and see all of its imperial attractions
in just three days? For most tourists, exploring the
island and visiting its most outstanding tourist
offerings in three days can be a tall order. With
dozens of bewitching tourist traps on display, a

three-day trip to this Mediterranean Eden may not be enough for some Santorini visitors. But with the right travel itinerary, a three-day trip to this island may be the most unforgettable and remarkable vacation in your life.

For your first stop, make your way to Fira, the largest and most crowded town in all of Santorini. Here, you may catch up on the fascinating and kaleidoscopic culture of Cyclades as well as learn more about the island's amusing history. Then, make a quick journey to Kamari, and gaze on the imposing ruins of the Ancient Thira. Can get enough of the island's historic and cultural offerings? Go to the Cultural Village of Pyrgos, and wander around its maze of beauty, before returning to Fira.

When the sun starts go down, follow the path to Oia, and catch a glimpse of its legendary romantic sunsets. Afterwards, head back to Fira for an exciting night of gourmet dining and cultural immersion.

Experience Fira's romantic vibe

A blissful way to start a phenomenal trip to this Mediterranean tourist hub is to take a leisurely stroll along the breathtaking caldera edge of Fira. Layered with infinity pools, cave apartments, upscale hotels and world-class restaurants, Fira's caldera edge boasts a nostalgic and dramatic vibe, giving you a taste of the mythical island Atlantis.

What's more, the place is crammed with spectacular sights and panoramic ocean views.

Additional information

- The best time to enjoy Fira's romantic scenery is between 7am to 9am. During these hours, the town's streets aren't crowded with tourists and locals.

Enjoy a toothsome snack

Feeling hungry already? Craving for something sweet and delicious? If your answer is a resounding 'yes', make a quick stop to Santorini Bakery Patisserie Pastry Lixoudis. Billed as the finest and most popular bakery on the island, the Santorini Bakery Patisserie Pastry Lixoudis will gratify your sweet tooth with its nectarous home-made ice cream, cookies, cake pops, baklava, pies and sugared almonds.

Additional information:

- Address: Fira 84700 Fira, Kikladhes, Greece

- Opening hours: Daily from 9:00am to 10:00pm

- Contact number: +30 694 799 6209

- Recommended time of arrival: Between 9am to 9:30am

Learn more about Thira's gripping ancient history

Step back in time, and find out what the island of Thira looked liked during the prehistoric era at the Museum of Prehistoric Thera. As you wander around the museum, you get to lay your eyes on a cluster of domestic artifacts that depict the lives of the people on the island before the great ancient earthquake. The visual highlight of this museum is the gleaming golden ibex figurine, which is in incredibly mint condition, even though it was made in 17th century BC. Also, don't forget to get a close look at the caldera's fossilized leaves of olive trees from 60,000 BC.

Additional information:

- Address: Mitropoleos Street, Fira 84700, Greece

- Contact number: +30 228 602 3217

- Admission fee: 3 EUR

- Opening hours: 8:30am to 3:00pm from Tuesday to Sunday

- Recommended time of arrival: Between 9am to 10am

The museum isn't open for business on Mondays. So, if your day one happens to fall on a Monday, look for a way to instill this visit to the other days of your Thira trip. To be honest, no trip to this island is complete without a stop to this museum. Besides, it is one of the island's most beloved gems and tourist traps.

A sneak peek of the island's old traditions

Lay fingers on the thought-provoking traditions of Santorini by visiting the Lignos Folklore Museum. Housed in a classic glazing Cyclades home, this museum showcases an interesting collection that brings to light the cultures of the island's dwellers and their everyday life during the 19th and 20th centuries. Aside from its striking and insightful exhibits, the museum also flaunts a ton of sylvan furniture, a wine pressing room, and a gorgeous church.

Additional information:

- Address: Kontochori, Fira 84700, Greece

- Contact number: +30 228 602 2792

- Admission fee: 3 EUR for adults. Free for children.

- Opening hours: 10am to 2pm, and 6 to 8pm.

- Recommended time of arrival: 10:30 to 11am

This folklore museum, however, only operates from April to October. Can't visit Thira during these months? Consider the museum mentioned below.

A modest cultural center housed in a resplendent building

Fostered inside a beautiful neo-classical home, the Megaro Gyzi Museum is an unpretentious treasury that houses enthralling pictures of Fira before and after the calamitous earthquake in 1956. Likewise, it displays a multitude of 15th century manuscripts, paintings and engravings. Established in 1980, this museum was designed to increase the cultural awareness of the island's occupants.

Additional information:

- Address: Fira 84700, Greece

- Contact number: +30 228 602 3077

- Admission fee: 3.5 EUR

- Opening hours: 10:30am to 1:30pm, and 5 to 8pm from Monday to Saturday. 10:30am to 4:30pm on Sundays.

- Recommended time of arrival: 10:30 to 11am

Take your lunch

With the first part of day 1 already in the books, it's time to reward yourself with a hearty and delectable meal at the Santo Mythos. Here, you get to choose from a wide variety of cheap yet delightful dishes, such as omelets, spaghetti, pizza, gyros, and a whole lot more.

- Address: M.Danezi Street, Fira, Greece

- Contact number: +30 228 602 1566

- Opening hours: 10am to 12am daily

- Recommended time of arrival: 11:45am to 12pm

An archeological delight in the heart of Santorini

Built in the 9th century BC by the Dorians (its first settlers), the Ancient Thira is truly a spectacle you cannot afford during your trip to Santorini. An absolute archeological delight, this iconic site is made up of awe-inspiring ruins from the Byzantine, Roman and Hellenistic periods. The remains of this site include a gymnasium, a theatre, an agora, temples as well as houses embellished with mosaics. To make your visit more pleasurable, the site has lovely scenery and offers amazing panoramic views of the island.

Additional information

- Address: Petros Nomikos Conference Center, Ancient Thera Road, Kamari 17892, Greece

- Contact number: +30 228 602 3217

- Admission fee: 4 EUR

- Opening hours: 8am to 2:30pm

- Recommended time of arrival: 12:30 to 2pm

To reach this tourist hot spot, first you need to travel to Kamari through a shuttle bus or a taxi cab. There are bus trips to Kamari from Fira's central square, Plateia Theotokopoulou, on a daily basis.

From Kamari, you will have to take a short yet steep trek to the site. Don't know what time Fira's public buses head off to Kamari? Check out this webpage:

http://ktel-santorini.gr/ktel/index.php/en/services-eng/timetable-summer-eng/list/15

A memento of the island's former grandeur

Pyrgos village of Santorini. Photo credit: *Klearchos Kapoutsis*

With its tiny neo-classical mansions, suave winding paths and old world charm, it is no wonder hordes of tourists flock to the Cultural Village in Pyrgos. A melting pot of Greek culture, the village has a network of alleys dotted with historic buildings, churches, shops, cafes and houses. As you reach the top of its mountain, you'll get bird's eye views of Perissa, the Ancient Thira and the rest of Kamari.

Also, you get to see and touch the remains of the Kastellia Castle. The best thing about this cultural adventure is that you get to enjoy it without spending a dime.

Additional information

- Address: Pyrgos 84701, Greece

- Contact number: +30 228 603 1101

- Admission fee: Free

- Recommended time of arrival: 3 to 4pm

From Kamari, you may reach this tranquil Greek village with a rented car using the directions shared at

http://www.distancesfrom.com/gr/directions-from-Kamari-to-pyrgos-village-santorini/DirectionHistory/4068377.aspx

Apart from private cars, you may also access this village with a public bus at Fira's bus station.

Enjoy Oia's famed majestic sunsets

Once you are in Fira, follow the path to the north of the town of Oia, and enjoy a few minutes of walking on its photographic cliff-top. Also, don't forget to explore the area's radiant village backstreets. As soon as you've reach Oia, find a good place to watch and take snapshots of Oia's beloved and splendid sunsets.

Dining options

As the island's capital, Fira is home to a bunch of ethereal taverns and upscale restaurants. Furthermore, the town has a wide range of cuisines, ranging from traditional Mediterranean dishes to classic American staples. Besides Fira, you may dine at any of the numerous upscale restaurants in Oia as well.

An evening of fine wine and quality entertainment

Looking for a great way to end a perfect day of cultural immersion in Santorini? After enjoying a filling dinner in Fira, take time to watch "The Greek Wedding Show" in The White Door Theatro. Heralded as the most illustrious cultural Greek show on the island, The Greek Wedding Show is a delightful one-of-a-kind spectacle composed of talented Greek actors and dancers. A psychedelic Greek fiesta, the show also entails you to savor sparkling wines as well as luscious mezedes and tapas.

Additional information

- Address: Fira 84700, Greece

- Contact number: +30 228 602 1770

- Price: 45 EUR

- Opening hours: 9pm

- Recommended time of arrival: 9pm

For bookings and reservations, visit their official website at:

http://www.whitedoorsantorini.com/english/home

3 BREATHTAKING OUTDOOR TRIPS AND MORE!

Red Beach of Santorini. Photo credit: <u>Klearchos Kapoutsis</u>

After a successful day of cultural immersion in Santorini, it's time for you to enjoy the outdoors and the island's unique volcanic beaches. For the first part of your second day of your trip to Thira, you will have to choose a beach destination or bay to suit your mood. Also, you have to choose the activities that you want to do on the beach or bay. Will it be cliff jumping on Amour Bay or a lazy morning at Kamari Beach, snacking at its bar, bathing under the sun and diving into its water for a snorkel? No matter what your choice is, rest assured your second day will be blissful and relaxing one.

On the afternoon, you will be taking a magical sunset cruise along the beautiful sapphire waters of Cyclades. Furthermore, you are going to explore the volcanic carter's rim from areas where the volcanic layers are most visible. Then, cap off your second day with an intoxicating night of partying and dining on the island's clutch of clubs, bars, restaurants and tavernas.

Can't decide which best is ideal for you? Take note of these pieces of information about the island's most prestigious beaches.

Red Beach

Of all the stunning beaches in Thira, the Red Beach is probably the most impressive and intriguing one. A classic exemplar of a volcanic beach, the Red Beach not only has stunning red volcanic sands, but it also has a reddish backdrop of towering sedimentary iron-rich rocks. What's more, it has crystal clear blue waters that add more appeal to its majestic beach setting. While the Red Beach can get a bit crowded, it is still a fascinating destination worth visiting. Not to mention, the beach can be accessed by any tourist for free.

Besides swimming, there are a couple of things you

may enjoy in this one-of-a-kind Greek beach. For one, you may kick back on its sands, relax and soak under the sun. Likewise, it is a great venue for snorkeling, as its waters are abundant with sea life.

Additional information

-   Address: Akrotiri, Greece

-   For conservative couples and families, the Red Beach might not your ideal respite since women here are usually topless.

-   Admission fee is free

-    To get there, first you need to hop on a bus from Fira bound for Akroiti. From there, you will have to take a boat ride that will take you to the beach. This boat ride usually cost 5 EUR.

-   Recommended time of arrival: 8am

Kamari

Kamari is truly the trendiest and most upscale beach in all of Santorini. An award-winning Greek beach, Kamari is famous for its pebbly terrain and long stretch of black and powdery sands. Furthermore, the beach has pleasant winds, friendly little waves and immaculately clean waters. Lined with beautiful thatched umbrellas, this beach can be a great place to relax, unwind and get away from the hustle bustle city life. Besides relaxing under the sun, the beach offers a plethora of intoxicating beach activities, such as kayaking, snorkeling and jet skiing. Looking for a heavy dose of fun and adventure in Kamari? Try diving towards at the hill near the Prophitis Ilias.

Additional information

- Address: Kamari, Greece

- As the island's most developed and sought after resorts, Kamari is home to a number of shops, beachfront bars, hotels and restaurants like Almira, Atmosphere Lounge and No Name.

- Admission fee is free.

- Getting there won't be a problem, as it can be easily accessed by bus and car.

- Recommended time of arrival: 8am

Amouri Bay

The Amouri Bay is a small magical cove with deep waters and a lot of colorful sea creatures. Encircled with rugged steep cliffs, this charming fishing area boasts a plethora of quaint tavernas, serving the freshest seafood in town. Moreover, it is a great vantage point to enjoy Oia's sunsets as well as enjoy superb views of the caldera.

Additional information

- Address: Oia, Greece
- Admission fee is free.

- How to get there? From northern end of Oia, you need to descend down around 300 steps. This hike might be taxing for some, but it is definitely worth a visit.

- Technically, Amoudi bay isn't a beach, but it is certainly the best spot to swim and take a splash.

- Be careful of the rocks, and wear the appropriate footwear.

- Recommended time of arrival: 8am

After spending a few hours on the beach, make your way to Fira's old port, for your next journey, which is a sailing cruise. This exciting adventure usually takes five hours and starts at 3 o'clock in the afternoon. If you have left the beach early, you may take short snap on your hotel, or do some shopping on the cobbled streets of Fira.

A spellbinding sailing cruise

Do you have an adventurous soul? Are looking for a way to deeply connect with the unique history of this volcanic Mediterranean island? Sail off to Santorini's deep blue waters on a cruise that features breathtaking and stunning views of the island's water-filled caldera as well as the radiant golden sun submerging into the sea.

From the Fira's old port, board on a sailing cruise that will take you to the Nea Kameni volcano. As the boat journeys on the calm blue waters of the Aegean sea, you will be treated with amazing views of the sunset. Upon your arrival at the iconic volcanic, a tour guide will then accompany you to several vantage points where you can feast your eyes on the caldera's steep and impressive inner walls. After this delightful sightseeing stop, your boat transverses to the volcano's hot springs and its thermal sulfurous waters, in which you take soothing and therapeutic bath.

Nea Kameni Volcano. Photo credit: <u>Stanisa Naumovski</u>

For the remainder of your voyage, the sail cruise will dock to Thirassia, a modest and vivid Cycladic island near Thira. As you enjoy the island's refreshing and crystal clear blue waters, the crew prepares a filling traditional Greek buffet. After your dinner, the boat will take you back you to Fira.

Tour operators

Bella Aurora & Thalassa

Where to get this tour? There are several options,

as far as operator goes. But, it is strongly recommended to book this tour from Bella Aurora & Thalassa. Awarded with a certificate of excellence in 2014 by Trip Advisor, the Bella Aurora & Thalassa is indeed the best operator to offer this kind of tour. Plus, their daily schedule fits perfectly to your travel itinerary.

- Address: Imerovigli-Santorini, Imerovigil 84700, Greece

- Contact number: +30 228 602 4024

- Website: http://www.santorini-cruises.com/

- Price: 56 EUR

- Inclusions: Entrance fee for the volcano, Meze (a Greek dish), local wines

- Make sure bring sweater or jacket, sunscreen lotion, swimwear, towel, hat and hiking shoes.

- By the way, the tour guide shares essential and captivating information about the volcano and the surrounding islands of Santorini.

There are several operators that provide personalized cruise tours toThirassia and Nea Kamini Volcano. Here's a list of some of the trusted operators for cruise tours in Santorini.

Brama Catamarans Sailing Cruises

- Address: Oia 84700, Greece

- Contact number: +30 697 797 7578

- Website: http://www.boatsingreece.com/

Santorini Sailing Center

- Address: Imerovigli 84700, Greece

- Contact number: +30 228 602 1370

- Website:
  http://www.sailingsantorini.gr/main.php

Santorini Yachting S/Y Eleftheria

- Address: Vlychada Marina, Vlychada
  84700, Greece

- Contact number: +30 694 441 0017

Website: http://www.sy-eleftheria.com/

4 A RIP-ROARING NIGHT OF PARTYING ON THE ISLAND

Koo Club, Santorini. Photo credit: John Y. Can

Tourists, for the most part, come to the island Santorini to relax, unwind and get away from the hectic city life. A peaceful and picturesque respite in the midst of the Aegean Sea, Thira's magic is induced by its riveting mythology, nature, history and, of course, irresistible views. But, there is a wild side to this somewhat quaint Mediterranean hub. When the sun goes in Santorini, the island marvelously transforms into a vivid party capital buzzing with cocktail lounges, upscale clubs and energetic bars with heart-pounding live music.

Looking for a great place to chill or party at night in Santorini? Make sure to take note of these suggestions and tips.

Groove Bar Kamari: A Cool And Unpretentious Sports Bar

Located right at the heart of Kamari, the Groove Bar Kamari is an astounding sports bar that offers live coverage of the world's most prestigious sporting events, such as the FIFA World Cup, NBA Finals, Tour De France, Moto GP and a whole lot more. Operated by a warm and courteous British couple, the bar also plays blistering hits from its extensive music library. On top of it all, the bar serves great tasting locally brewed beers, such as Red Donkey Ale and Yellow Donkey ale.

Additional information:

- Address: Po Box number 5544, Kamari, Greece

- Contact number: +30 228 603 0433

- Opening hours: 11am to 2am

- Website: http://groovebarkamari.com/

Koo Club: The Hottest Dance Club on the island

Are you in mood for dancing? Do you love cocktails

and electrifying electronic music? Well, Fira's Koo Club has a plethora of these nightlife offerings. Often called as the best nightclub in Cyclades, Koo Club sets your night on fire with its lavish sofas, and heart-pounding techno music from the island's best DJs. What's more, it has a long chic bar that serves high-end cocktails and alcoholic drinks.

- Address: Fira 847 00, Santorini, Greece

- Contact number: +30 228 602 2025

- Opening hours: 10pm to 5a, daily from July to August.

- Website: http://www.kooclub.gr/

Enigma Club: One Of The Oldest Nightspots In Thira

Established in summer of 1979, Enigma Club has been a staple in Satorini's vibrant nightlife scene. One of the most sought after nightlife venues on the island, Enigma Club beckons party animals with its spacious dance clubs, lavish rooms, and pulsating techno dance beats. As for its overall design, the club has lavish Cycladic decorations of tiled floors and stone-encrusted walls coupled with lighten palm trees.

Additional information:

- Address: Main Square, Fira, Santorini, Greece

- Contact number: +30 228 602 2466

- Opening hours: 12am to 5am on Fridays and Saturdays

Lioyerma Lounge Café Pool Bar: A Calm And Relaxing Oasis

For a relaxing night out in Santorini, go to Lioyerma Lounge Café Pool Bar in Oia. A cushy and tranquil oasis, Lioyerma Lounge Café Pool Bar gives you amazing views of the Aegean Sea and the caldera. In addition, it has a clean swimming pool where you enjoy delightful island drinks and special cocktails.

Additional information:

- Address: Oia 84702, Santorini, Greece

- Contact number: +30 228 607 1190

- Webiste: http://www.lioyerma.gr/

Tango Bar: A Glamorous Bar With A Twist

Often ranked as one of the top nightspots in Santorini, the Tango Bar is a glamorous bar perched on the Fira's Cliffside. Besides its great dramatic caldera views, this opulent bar also has top-notch service as well as serves fresh fruity cocktails and tasty champagnes. As a premier Mediterranean nightspot, the place is indeed a terrific place to chill out and catch up with friends. But, as the night progresses, the venue becomes a peppy club with flocks of party animals dancing to the DJ's dynamic beats.

- Address: Marinatou Street, Fira Old Port, Santorini, Greece

- Contact number: +30 697 449 8206

- Opening hours: 9:30pm to 5am

- Website: http://www.tangosantorini.gr/

Kira Thira: An Intimate Jazz Bar

Looking for cool and soothing jazz music in Santorini? Then, Kira Thira is your best bet. One of the finest and oldest bars in Fira, Kira Thira is quite popular among international travelers and locals, thanks to its smooth jazz music. Plus, it has vaulted and dark wood ceilings, adding more intimacy to its laid-back atmosphere.

- Address: Erythrou Stavrou, Fira, Santorini, Greece

- Contact number: +30 228 602 2770

- Opening hours: 9pm to 6am from Wednesday to Sunday

Additional Tips

If you are planning to visit this island in July, make sure to participate in their highly acclaimed annual music event, the Santorini Jazz Festival. Since 1997, this exciting music event has been assembling trendy and skilled jazz artists and musicians from all over the world. Also, in August, the island becomes a host to another music festival, the Santorini Music Festival.

5 AN UNFORGETTABLE WINE TOUR COUPLED WITH A EUPHORIC SHOPPING EXPERIENCE

Santorini - At Santo Wines. Photo credit: Stefani Friedrich

Are you a wine connoisseur? Do you love sampling sumptuous world-class wines? Then, take a 4-hour wine tour around the island, and get a taste of its famed wine varietals. Led by an omniscient wine expert, this wine tour will take you to three of the best and most sought-after traditional wineries on the island. As you take this 4-hour tour, you'll get to witness how the process of winemaking unfolds, from the harvesting of grapes to maturing the wine. Best of all, you get to sample a dozen of different Santorini wines along with a platter of local Greek delicacies. In the wake of a blissful wine tour, you will be heading to Oia, to buy souvenirs and unique gift items. Does this sound fun to you?

Why should I take a wine tour?

Producing some of Greece's most beloved wines, the island of Santorini is a host to several exquisite traditional wineries. Furthermore, Santorini has a dazzling variety of rare and distinct wines, thanks to the volcanic soil's mineral content and island's unique climate. Even if you are not fond of wines, taking tour is still an absolute must. Why? Because this tour allows you to savor an array of tasty local treats, experience the countryside charm of Santorini, as well as lay eyes on its beautiful landscapes.

Highlights and features of the tour

- The tour starts with a pickup at your hotel.

- The tour, usually, starts at 10:30 in the morning and ends at 2:30 in the afternoon.

- You will be traveling in a cozy and relaxing fashion with an air-conditioned minibus.

- The tour features a tour guide that provides all his or her experience and knowledge pertaining to the island's fine wines.

- Visit three award-winning traditional wineries on the island.

- A leisurely walk around an intriguing volcanic vineyard, and an insight about Santorini's unique viticulture.

- Enjoy a dozen or more popular wine varietals, such as Vinsanto, Nykteri, and Assyrtiko.

- Balance out or complement the flavors of the served wine with delectable local delicacies that include olives, bread, salami and cheese.

- After the four-hour trip, you will be escorted back to your hotel or any venue in Fira.

Wineries

The wineries included in this tour vary from one tour operator to another. In addition, some tour operators allow their guests to pick the wineries that they want to visit. Below are the best and most popular wineries in this picturesque Greek island.

Koutsoyannopoulos Wine Museum

No wine tour on the island of Santorini is complete without a stop to the Koutsoyannopoulos Wine Museum. In this museum, tourists get to discover the island's rich history of wineries and vineyards. A labyrinth of winemaking history, this museum has audio guides that give you a chance to learn more about the island's winemaking industry from the 1660s to today.

- Address: Vothonas, Santorini, Greece

- Contact number: +30 228 603 1322

Santo Wines

Santo Wines is arguably the best winery in all of Thira. Not only is it filled with local food specialties and wines, but is also boast fantastic views of the caldera and cliffs.

- Address: Pyrgos, Santorini, Greece

- Contact number: + 30 228 602 8056

Boutari

Boutari is the largest winery on the island. In addition, it has one of the oldest vineyards in the country.

- Address: Megalochiri, Santorini, Greece

- Contact number: +30 228 608 1011

Gavalas Winery

For hundreds of years, this winery has strived to produce the best tasting wines from the grapes that are indigenous to the island. Located on a dramatic cliff near Megalochori, a visit to this renowned winery gives you a lasting gulp of the island's winemaking industry with its charming vineyards and wine museum.

- Address: Megalochori, Santorini, Greece
- Contact number: + 30 228 608 2552

Tour operators

There are a few tour operators on the island that offer wine tours to all the island's guests. To help you choose a good and reliable operator for your wine tour, consider these suggestions:

Santorini Wine Tour

- Address: Vourvoulos, Fira, Greece
- Contact number: +30 693 708 4958
- Price: 75 EUR
- Website: http://www.santoriniwinetour.com/

Santorini Wine Adventure Tours

- Address: Fira, Santorini, Greece
- Contact number: +30 693 296 0062
- Price: 70 EUR
- Website: http://www.winetoursantorini.com/

SAFOWI Santorini Food and Wine Tours

- Address: Oia 84702, Greece

- Contact number: +30 228 607 1474

- Price: 120 EUR

- Website: http://www.safowi.com/safowi-tours.html

Shopping Time!

A lot of tourists in Santorini enjoy spending a small portion of their vacation in shopping. As the island's visitor, shopping is truly a great way to meet and mingle with the Santorini's businesses and locals, allowing you to learn more about the Cyclades history and culture. At the same time, shopping allows to acquire new belongings that commemorate your trip to this Greek Elysium. Plus, Santorini has a myriad of unique items that are sold at very affordable and reasonable rates.

Where to shop?

Fira is by far the best place to shop on the island of Santorini. As the island's capital and main business district, the bustling Greek town has rustic cobblestone streets buzzing with shops and boutiques that offer endless shopping options. At the town's centers, shopping will be amazed with the sheer number of lavish boutiques and jewelry shops. Can't afford to buy jewelry and other luxurious products? Go to the main square, and look for shops that sell regular souvenirs like hats, postcards and shirts.

Oia is also a good place to shop for souvenirs and rare items. In this lovely Greek town, tourist will find a number of art shops that sell sensational Greek paintings. Likewise, it has a handful of stores that offer beautiful and high quality ceramics.

6 BEST PLACES TO DINE IN THIRA

Seafood at Selene restaurant in Fira, Santorini. Photo credit: bongo vongo

Craving for something spicy and sweet? Looking for a healthy traditional Mediterranean dish? Whatever your palate is, the island of Santorini has something delicious in store for you. As one of the world's most popular honeymoon destinations, Thira has become a home to a colony of world-class restaurants and tavernas. From pizzas to traditional homemade food, these dining centers offer a wide variety of delightful and hearty cuisines. Indeed, a trip to this Mediterranean island is a satisfying gastronomic journey that pleases your taste buds and stomach.

But with so many options to choose from, how do you pick the best places to dine in Santorini? Luckily for you, this guide contains loads of information pertaining to the finest restaurants on the island.

Cheap options

Terr Nera

A small restaurant nestled on Perivolos Beach, Terra Nera delights its guests with its nectarous waffles, hearty pizzas, cool smoothies, frozen yogurts and hamburgers. Additionally, it has efficient service and boasts a scenic ambiance.

- Address: Perivolos Beach, Santorini, Greece

- Contact number: +30 228 677 1511

To Pinako

In spite of its relatively small size, a lot of foodies consider To Pinako as one of the finest restaurants in all of Santorini. After all, it is a first-rate Greek restaurant that specializes in serving Santorian meze. As for their drinks, this restaurant serves sumptuous traditional Greek liquors.

- Address: Kamari 84700, Santorini, Greece

- Contact number: +30 228 603 2280

Sky Lounge

Boasting a romantic setting and great views of the Aegean Sea, the Sky Lounge has been a favorite among romantic couples and lovers. As a matter of fact, it is one of the best places on the island to hold a wedding reception. Aside from its dramatic and idyllic setting, the restaurant also serves delectable chicken kebab and other barbecued treats. Moreover, it offers delicious strawberries and affordable champagnes.

- Address: Kamari Beach, Kamari, Santorini, Greece

- Contact number: +30 693 941 8960

Medium range

To Psaraki

Longing for seafood? To Psaraki is a Mediterranean seaside taverna known for its fresh seafood and tasty local specialties, such as their yummy white aubergine filed stuffed with tomatoes. To add more flavor to your meal, you may order their lovely local white wine.

- Address: Vlychada Marina, Vlychada 847010, Santorini, Greece

- Contact number: +30 228 608 2783

Katharos Lounge

Katharos Lounge is certainly one of the most

underrated restaurants on the island. A picturesque lounge with great views of the Aegean Sea, this Mediterranean restaurant raptures you, as their guest, with its healthy Greek dishes, wonderful atmosphere and excellent music.

- Address: Katharos Beach, Oia, Santorini, Greece

- Contact number: +30 687 096 6754

Paradox Thai Food & Bar

Quench your cravings for spicy Asian munchies by indulging in the traditional Thai staples served at Paradox Thai Food & Bar. A breath of fresh on the island's culinary scene, this restaurant offers succulent and nutritious Thai dishes like green curry and chicken noodles.

- Address: Oia 84702, Santorini, Greece

- Contact number: +30 228 607 1675

Splurge

Sea Side by Notos

An award-winning restaurant, the Sea Side by Notos is a trendy and cozy restaurant with a huge selection of fresh seafood. In addition, it offers a whole lot of delicious Greek dishes with a contemporary twist. A must-try in this restaurant is the Moussaka.

- Address: Agios Georgios Beach, Perivolos, Santorini, Greece

- Contact number: +30 228 608 2801

Kapari Wine Restaurant

Looking for a restaurant with scenic views and premium quality wines? Then, head off to Kapari Wine Restaurant. Spearheaded by the up-and-coming chef George Belesis, this classy restaurant will amuse with its contemporary dishes like the delightful pumpkin soup with cooked shrimp.

- Address: City Street, Imerovigli, Santorini, Greece

- Contact number: +30 228 602 1120

Selene

Selene is a charming and unpretentious Greek restaurant that will leave you speechless. Billed as one of the best restaurants in all Greece, this restaurant defines fine Greek dining with its eclectic menu and unusual yet delicious Greek dishes.

- Address: Pyrgos 84700, Santorini, Greece

- Contact number: +30 228 602 2249

A word of advice

Thira's cuisine is mainly based on its own produce and agricultural products. With the sea breeze of the Aegean Sea and volcanic soils on the island, these agricultural products give their dishes a unique and flavorful dish. To savor the island's tasty culture, make sure to sample their traditional dishes, such as saffron bread rusks, sweet melitinia, brantada, stuffed round courgettes, omelette and white aubergines.

7 WHERE TO SLEEP IN SANTORINI?

Path to hotel Keti of Santorini. Photo credit: Bhakti Dharma

There is no shortage of accommodations on the island of Santorini. From luxurious resorts and cave hotels to budget hotels, the island has an assortment of accommodations to suit any kind of traveler. Whether you are a budget-conscious traveler or a newlywed looking for romantic views of the island, Santorini has a hotel to suit your preferences and budget.

Finding the right place to stay on the island, though, can be a bit overwhelming, with the numerous options available. Fortunately, this guide has a plethora of information regarding the best accommodations in Thira. To help you choose best places to crash on the island, take note of the suggestions and hints listed below.

Budget friendly options

Villa Anemone

Located right at the heart of Santorini, Villa Anemone gives its guests easy access to some of the island's most famous landmarks and attractions, including the Santorini Folklore Museum, the Museum of Prehistoric Thira and Agios Nikalaos Monastery. What's more, this guesthouse boasts a ton of premium amenities, such as ticket and tour assistance, concierge services as well as complimentary internet access.

- Address: Main Street, Fira 84700, Greece

- Contact number: +30 228 602 3681

Pension George

A backpacker's delight, Pension George is one of the best and most affordable guesthouses in all of Cyclades. In fact, it has been recommended by a handful of online guides, such as Rough Guide and Frommers. It has a warm and friendly atmosphere coupled with a ton of amazing amenities and facilities.

- Address: Thera 84700, Greece

- Contact number: +30 228 602 2351

Keti Hotel

Enjoying astounding views of the Aegean Sea, Keti Hotel is a charming and picturesque hotel that features a breathtaking traditional Cycladic architectural design. Moreover, it has air-conditioned rooms that come with a slew of amenities, such as televisions with satellite channels, free toiletries and a whole lot more.

- Address: Fira 84700, Santorini, Greece

- Contact number: +30 228 602 2324

Medium range accommodations

Santorini's Balcony Art Houses

Santorini's Balcony Art Houses is a stunning hotel nestled on Imerovigli's famous caldera. Known for its amazing ambiance and great value, the hotel is also famous for its luxurious facilities, including an outdoor with poolside bar and hydro-massage section, as well as a gorgeous sunbathing terrace that feature views of the cliff's edge and the volcano.

- Address: Oias Road, Imerovigli, Santorini, Greece

- Contact number: +30 228 602 3743

Manos Small World

Looking for a relaxing place to get a good night's sleep in Santorini? With its elegant suites, unhindered sea views and panoramic terrace, the Manos Small World gives you a peaceful and relaxing haven during your trip to Thira. Aside from its opulent setting, the hotel features spacious and cozy suites with premium beds, LCD televisions, designer toiletries and a lot of other amenities.

- Address: Main Street Firostefani, Santorini, Greece

- Contact number: +30 228 602 2091

Residence Suites

One of the most stylish hotels in Santorini, Residence Suites delights its guests with its splendid collection of decorated studios and suites on top of Oia's cliff. As a guest in this hotel, you get to enjoy awe-inspiring views of the sea from a private balcony or terrace. In addition, each room as has a hairdryer, television with satellite and cable channels, as well as air conditioning.

- Address: Main Street, Oia, Santorini 84702, Greece

- Contact number: +30 228 607 1406

Lavish accommodations

Perivolas Hotel

A five-star world-class hotel, Perivolas Hotel is truly the ultimate caldera accommodation in Santorini. Billed as one of the top and premier hotels in Greece, Perivolas Hotel features intimate and inviting rooms with kitchenettes, individual terraces and vaulted ceilings. Not to mention, it has a stockpile of amenities and facilities, such as an infinity pool, restaurant, bar and wellness studio.

- Address: Oia, Santorini, Greece

- Contact number: +30 228 607 1308

Santorini Secret

Perched on the volcanic rocks of Oia, Santorini Secret is a ritzy five-start boutique hotel that offers well-decorated suites with hot tubs and private pools overlooking the volcano and caldera. In addition, it boasts a first-class restaurant and an infinity pool.

- Address: Oia, 84702, Santorini, Greece

- Contact number: +30 2286 602 7337

Kapari Natural Resort

With its prime location and great views of the caldera, it is no wonder this five-star complex gets a bunch of positive reviews from a lot of tourists. Aside from its excellent location and amazing vibes, Kapari Natural Resort also beautiful traditional rooms with state-of-the-art amenities, including Wi-Fi, flat HDTVs and more.

- Address: Thera 84700, Santorini, Greece

- Contact number: +30 228 602 1120

CONCLUSION

Oia, Santorini. Photo credit: <u>*hans-johnson*</u> *CC BY-ND*

From romantic couples to adventurous souls, the magical island of Santorini beckons millions of international tourists with its eclectic collection of tourist traps and attractions. Known as one of the most romantic destinations in the world, Santorini boasts a romantic vibe coupled with breathtaking views of the Aegean Sea and caldera. What's more, it has a wealth of gorgeous Cyclades buildings, adding to its natural appeal. For history buffs, Santorini's intrigue extends deep into its past with

Oia's gorgeous traditional hilltop village, and Akrotiri's enchanting Minoa site. On top of it all, it has excellent wineries, world-class restaurants and multi-colored sandy beaches.

There are a lot of cool and exciting things to do within 72 hours in this idyllic Greek dreamland. Whether you are a wine lover or someone who loves sightseeing, a three-day vacation on this island will definitely give you a trip of a lifetime. If, however, you cannot get enough of Thira in 72 hours, extend your vacation, and explore the other majestic tourist magnets of the island. Αντιο!

MORE FROM THIS AUTHOR

Below you'll find some of our other books that are popular on Amazon and Kindle as well. Alternatively, you can visit our author page on Amazon to see other work done by us.

3 Day Guide to Berlin: A 72-hour definitive guide on what to see, eat and enjoy in Berlin, Germany

3 Day Guide to Vienna: A 72-hour definitive guide on what to see, eat and enjoy in Vienna Austria

3 Day Guide to Santorini: A 72-hour definitive guide on what to see, eat and enjoy in Santorini Greece

3 Day Guide to Provence: A 72-hour definitive guide on what to see, eat and enjoy in Provence, France

3 Day Guide to Istanbul: A 72-hour definitive guide on what to see, eat and enjoy in Istanbul, Turkey

3 Day Guide to Budapest: A 72-hour Definitive Guide on What to See, Eat and Enjoy in Budapest, Hungary

3 Day Guide to Venice: A 72-hour Definitive Guide on What to See, Eat and Enjoy in Venice, Italy

Printed in Great Britain
by Amazon

34894590R00038